PATRICK KANE

HOCKEY SUPERSTAR

BY WILL GRAVES

First Edition
First Printing, 2019

Book design by Jake Nordby
Cover design by Jake Nordby
Photographs ©: Mike Wulf/Cal Sport Media/ZUMA Wire/AP Images, cover, 1, back cover; Christopher Szagola/Icon Sportswire, 4, 30; Matt Slocum/AP Images, 6, 8–9, 21; Claus Andersen/Getty Images Sport/Getty Images, 10; Anders Wiklund/Scanpix Sweden/AP Images, 13; Charles Rex Arbogast/AP Images, 15; Mark Humphrey/AP Images, 16–17; Brian Kersey/UPI/Newscom, 19; Michael Tureski/Icon Sportswire, 22; Robin Alam/Icon Sportswire/AP Images, 25; Kamil Krzaczynski/AP Images, 26; Red Line Editorial, 29

Press Box Books, an imprint of Press Room Editions.

Library of Congress Control Number: 2019936727

ISBN
978-1-63494-099-3 (library bound)
978-1-63494-108-2 (paperback)
978-1-63494-117-4 (epub)
978-1-63494-126-6 (hosted ebook)

Distributed by North Star Editions, Inc.
2297 Waters Drive
Mendota Heights, MN 55120
www.northstareditions.com

Printed in the United States of America

About the Author

Will Graves has worked for more than two decades as a sports journalist. Since 2011 he has served as correspondent for the Associated Press in Pittsburgh, Pennsylvania.

TABLE OF CONTENTS

BAUER
FINAL
BAUER
88
BAUER

1 OVERTIME WINNER

Patrick Kane deked past a defenseman and raced down the left side of the ice. Kane and the Chicago Blackhawks were battling the Philadelphia Flyers in the 2010 Stanley Cup Final. Game 6 had gone to overtime with the score tied 3–3.

As Kane approached the net, the goalie seemed to be in good position. Kane didn't have much to shoot at as he skated just above the goal line. But the star right winger let the shot go anyway. Kane heard a clank as the puck smacked off

Patrick Kane skates with the puck during Game 6 of the 2010 Stanley Cup Final.

Kane and the Blackhawks celebrate a championship while the stunned Philadelphia crowd looks on.

the far post and bounced into the net. Then he took off sprinting. For a moment, nobody else in the arena knew what to do. Not the fans. Not the referees. Not even Kane's teammates. They didn't realize the puck was in the net.

But Kane knew. He raced down the ice in celebration. His overtime goal had lifted Chicago to a 4–3 victory. For the first time since 1961, the Blackhawks were champions of the National Hockey League (NHL).

It took a few seconds for everyone else to catch on. And maybe it's only fitting. Kane has always been ahead of the curve. His unforgettable overtime goal ended Chicago's five decades of misery. It also crowned Kane as one of the best hockey players of his generation.

MISSING PUCK

Kane's game-winning goal marked the 16th time the Stanley Cup Final ended with an overtime goal. But in this case, nobody seems to know what happened to the puck. In the chaos after Kane scored, no one kept track of it. Flyers defenseman Kimmo Timonen, who became Kane's teammate when he joined the Blackhawks in 2015, joked that he's still not sure the puck actually went into the net. History begs to differ.

THE CHAMPIONSHIP GOAL

Flyers goalie Michael Leighton looks for the puck, which ended up hidden in the corner of the net.

OHL
KNIGHTS
CCM
Oshawa
GENERALS
ONE90

2 PATH TO STARDOM

Patrick Kane was born in Buffalo, New York, on November 19, 1988. From an early age, he loved sports. It didn't matter if it was basketball, baseball, lacrosse, soccer, or hockey. Patrick was up for anything. But it soon became clear that his best sport was hockey. His blazing speed on the ice made him nearly unstoppable, even when he faced older players.

When Patrick was 14, he joined HoneyBaked, a developmental team based in Detroit, Michigan. He lived with

Patrick Kane (left) rarely had the height advantage, but he scored plenty of goals.

Hockey Hall of Famer Pat Verbeek. Patrick learned everything he could from Verbeek, who scored more than 500 goals during his long career in the NHL.

Verbeek told Patrick that even though he might be smaller than some of the other players, he didn't have to be afraid. Patrick took that lesson to heart. In his only season with HoneyBaked, he scored 83 goals in 70 games.

When Patrick was 16, he moved on to the USA Hockey National Team Development Program. But success didn't come easily. The first two times

SIBLING COMPROMISE

Growing up in Buffalo, Patrick wanted to play sports all the time. There was just one problem. His three younger sisters didn't always want to join him. So Patrick struck a deal with them. He would play dolls or house if they joined him for a game when they were done.

Kane (27) scores against Sweden during the 2007 World Junior Ice Hockey Championships.

he tried out for the national team, he didn't make it. Coaches were worried that he wasn't big enough.

Patrick kept at it. He finally made Team USA's Under-17 National Team in 2004. And right away, he wowed his teammates with his skill. In his second season with the team, he set a program record with 102 points.

In 2006, when Kane was nearly 18 years old, he joined the London Knights of the Ontario Hockey League. In just 58 games, he racked up 62 goals and 83 assists. Thanks to stats like that, he was named the league's rookie of the year. Kane was on his way to stardom.

In the 2007 NHL Entry Draft, the Chicago Blackhawks selected Kane with the first overall pick. The Blackhawks were one of the NHL's oldest teams. But they had fallen on hard times. Before selecting Kane, the Blackhawks had made the playoffs just once in the previous nine years.

Kane shows off his new Blackhawks sweater after being drafted by Chicago.

Chicago believed Kane had the talent to help turn the team around. His arrival did more than that. It put the Blackhawks on the path to become champions.

BAUER

3 CLIMBING TO THE TOP

Being the top pick in the draft comes with a ton of pressure. Patrick Kane's combination of speed and vision made him seem destined for stardom. He spent his first season living up to the hype.

It helped that he had a teammate who could keep up with him. Jonathan Toews had been drafted by the Blackhawks a year earlier. Chicago's coaches knew how important Kane and Toews were to the team's future. The club made sure they shared a hotel room on road trips, hoping

Kane and Toews celebrate after a goal against the Nashville Predators in 2009.

they would build a close friendship that paid off on the ice. They certainly did.

During Kane's rookie season, he ended up with 21 goals and 51 assists. He edged Toews to win the Calder Memorial Trophy, given each year to the NHL's top rookie. Still, it wasn't quite enough for the Blackhawks to make the playoffs. In his Calder acceptance speech, Kane promised Chicago would be back in the postseason soon.

He was right. In 2008–09, the Blackhawks had their best record in more than a decade. They finished second in the NHL's Central Division.

Though Kane was just 20 years old, he looked right at home in the playoffs. The Blackhawks cruised past the Calgary Flames in the opening round. Next they faced the

Kane works along the boards during a 2009 playoff game against the Canucks.

Vancouver Canucks. That's when Kane took his game to another level. He collected six goals in six games, including the first hat trick of his NHL career in Game 6.

Chicago's playoff run ended with a loss to the rival Detroit Red Wings. However, the team's strong play sent a warning to the rest of the NHL. The Blackhawks were back.

A year later, Kane and the rest of the team weren't just back. They were champions. Kane's goal in Game 6 of the 2010 Stanley Cup Final set off a massive party back in Chicago. Fans crammed the sidewalks to thank Kane and his teammates for bringing home the Blackhawks' first championship in 49 years. The wait for the next title wouldn't be nearly as long.

OLYMPIC STAR

The Stanley Cup wasn't the only hardware Kane brought home in 2010. He helped the United States win a silver medal at the 2010 Winter Olympics. Kane hurt his right knee before the start of the tournament, but it hardly slowed him down. He scored three goals and added two assists. That was the good news. The bad news? Kane and Team USA lost to Canada in the gold-medal game.

Kane hoists the Stanley Cup after his overtime goal in 2010.

BALL
Reebok

FINAL
NHL
NHL
NHL
NHL
NHL

4 MORE TITLES, MORE TROPHIES

The 2010 Stanley Cup proved to be just the beginning for Patrick Kane and the Blackhawks. Within a few years, championship parades had become a regular part of the Chicago sports calendar.

In 2013 Kane led the Blackhawks to the Stanley Cup Final once again. And although he couldn't match his dramatic finish in 2010, he didn't have to. Kane's two goals in Game 5 gave Chicago control of the series over the Boston Bruins. Then

Kane poses with the Conn Smythe Trophy after winning the Stanley Cup in 2013.

in Game 6, the Blackhawks stunned Boston with a thrilling come-from-behind victory late in the third period. For the second time in his career, Kane lifted the Stanley Cup.

A DAY WITH THE CUP

As part of the Stanley Cup celebration, each player on the winning team gets to spend a day with the Cup during the off-season. After winning the Cup in 2013, Kane took the trophy back to Buffalo. He shared it with members of the United States Air Force base in Niagara Falls, New York. He later took the Cup to his favorite pizza parlor near the home where he grew up.

Kane finished the 2013 playoffs with nine goals and ten assists. That earned him the Conn Smythe Trophy, which is given to the most valuable player of the postseason. Kane did his best to downplay the award. He said his teammates deserved as much credit as he did.

Kane and the Blackhawks weren't done yet. In 2015 they won their third Stanley Cup

Kane skates with the puck during Game 4 of the 2015 Stanley Cup Final.

in six seasons by beating the Tampa Bay Lightning. Kane once again found himself right in the middle of an important moment. His only goal of the Final came in Game 6.

Kane scores an easy goal against the Coyotes in 2019.

With just over five minutes to go, his one-timer gave the Blackhawks a 2–0 lead. Minutes later, he was celebrating on the ice as the home crowd roared.

The next season proved to be Kane's best yet. In 2016, he became the first American-born player to win the Hart Trophy. That award is given to the NHL's most valuable player. Kane's 106 points also led the NHL that season. He became the first American to capture the Art Ross Trophy, given to the league's top scorer.

The Blackhawks had disappointing seasons in both 2017–18 and 2018–19. Chicago failed to reach the playoffs two years in a row. However, Kane remained the team's leading point scorer. In fact, during the 2018–19 season, he scored more than 100 points for only the second time in his career.

Blackhawks fans had reason to remain hopeful. With Patrick Kane on the team, there was always a chance that Chicago would be celebrating another championship.

TIMELINE

1. **Buffalo, New York (November 19, 1988)**
   Patrick Kane is born in Buffalo, New York.

2. **London, Ontario (April 27, 2007)**
   Kane is named the Ontario Hockey League Rookie of the Year after scoring 62 goals and adding 83 assists in 58 games.

3. **Columbus, Ohio (June 22, 2007)**
   The Chicago Blackhawks select Kane with the first overall pick in the 2007 NHL Entry Draft.

4. **Saint Paul, Minnesota (October 4, 2007)**
   Kane makes his NHL debut with the Blackhawks, who fall 1–0 to the Minnesota Wild.

5. **Chicago, Illinois (May 11, 2009)**
   Kane collects the first hat trick of his NHL career in Game 6 of the Western Conference semifinals against the Vancouver Canucks.

6. **Vancouver, British Columbia (February 28, 2010)**
   Kane earns a silver medal while playing for Team USA at the 2010 Winter Olympics.

7. **Philadelphia, Pennsylvania (June 9, 2010)**
   Kane scores the championship-winning goal in Game 6 of the 2010 Stanley Cup Final.

8. **Las Vegas, Nevada (June 22, 2016)**
   Kane wins the Hart Trophy as the league's MVP, the Ted Lindsay Award as the most outstanding player as voted by the players, and the Art Ross Trophy as the NHL's top scorer.

MAP

AT-A-GLANCE

Birth date: November 19, 1988

Birthplace: Buffalo, New York

Position: Right wing

Shoots: Left

Size: 5 feet 10 inches, 177 pounds

NHL team: Chicago Blackhawks (2007–)

Previous teams: US Olympic team (2010, 2014), Detroit HoneyBaked (2003–04), USA Hockey National Development Team Program (2004–06), London Knights (2006–07)

Major awards: Calder Trophy (2008), Conn Smythe Trophy (2013), Hart Trophy (2016), Art Ross Trophy (2016), Ted Lindsay Award (2016), Stanley Cup champion (2010, 2013, 2015)

Accurate through the 2018–19 season.

GLOSSARY

assist
A pass that results in a goal.

deke
To fake a movement in a certain direction to confuse an opponent.

developmental team
A team that helps young players build their skills.

draft
An event that allows teams to choose new players coming into the league.

generation
A group of people who are all born around the same time.

hat trick
A game in which a player scores three or more goals.

one-timer
A shot that a player takes immediately after receiving a pass, without controlling the puck first.

playoffs
A set of games to decide a league's champion.

point
A statistic that a player earns by scoring a goal or having an assist.

rival
An opposing player or team that brings out the greatest emotion from fans and players.

TO LEARN MORE

Books

Gitlin, Marty. *Patrick Kane: Hockey Star.* Lake Elmo, MN: Focus Readers, 2017.

Page, Sam. *Hockey: Then to Wow!* New York: Time Inc. Books, 2017.

Peters, Chris. *Hockey Season Ticket: The Ultimate Fan Guide.* Mendota Heights, MN: Press Box Books, 2019.

Websites

Chicago Blackhawks Official Site
https://www.nhl.com/blackhawks

London Knights Official Site
http://londonknights.com

Team USA Official Site
https://teamusa.usahockey.com

INDEX